CONTE

C000215933

CHOICE

Emily Berry • *Unexhausted Time* • Faber

RECOMMENDATIONS

Will Alexander • *Refractive Africa* • Granta
Fiona Benson • *Ephemeron* • Cape
Warsan Shire • *Bless the Daughter Raised by a Voice in Her Head* • Chatto
Jessica Traynor • *Pit Lullabies* • Bloodaxe Books

SPECIAL COMMENDATION

Denise Riley • *Lurex* • Picador

TRANSLATION CHOICE

In the Same Light: 200 Tang Poems for our Century
Translated by Wong May • Carcanet

PAMPHLET CHOICE

Pip Osmond-Williams • *Of Algae & Grief* • Dempsey & Windle

WILD CARD

Jeremy Hooker • *The Release* • Shearsman Books

Poetry Book Society

CHOICE SELECTORS RECOMMENDATION SPECIAL COMMENDATION	SARAH HOWE & ANTHONY ANAXAGOROU
TRANSLATION SELECTOR	HARRY JOSEPHINE GILES
PAMPHLET SELECTORS	MARY JEAN CHAN & NICK MAKOHA
WILD CARD SELECTOR	CALEB FEMI
CONTRIBUTORS	SOPHIE O'NEILL NATHANIEL SPAIN KYM DEYN LEDBURY CRITICS
EDITORIAL & DESIGN	ALICE KATE MULLEN

Poetry Book Society Memberships

Choice
4 Books a Year: 4 Choice books & 4 *Bulletins* (UK £55, Europe £65, ROW £75)
World
8 Books: 4 Choices, 4 Translation books & 4 *Bulletins* (£98, £120, £132)
Complete
24 Books: 4 Choices, 16 Recommendations, 4 Translations & 4 *Bulletins* (£223, £265, £292)

Single copies of the *Bulletin* £9.99

Cover Art Édouard Bossé, Unsplash

Poetry Book Society | Milburn House | Dean Street | Newcastle upon Tyne | NE1 1LF
0191 230 8100 | enquiries@poetrybooksociety.co.uk

WWW.POETRYBOOKS.CO.UK

LETTER FROM THE PBS

Welcome to the Spring 2022 *Bulletin*. We at the Poetry Book Society are looking forward to getting out in the world and hope to see many of our readers, poets and contributors over the course of the year. We can be found mainly in the north this spring and hope to see you at StAnza poetry festival in St Andrews on the 13th March for readings from Emily Berry, Will Alexander and Fiona Benson, or at our local Newcastle Poetry Festival in May. Wherever you are, we hope you can celebrate poetry this year and we really hope you enjoy this season's selections.

Emily Berry is the Spring Choice with the outstanding *Unexhausted Time,* described by selector Anthony Anaxagorou, "as majestic as it is impressive". The scope of the further recommendations and selections is immense, from the Tang dynasty to Greek myth, African post-colonial empowerment, anxiety of parenthood, notions of family, the body; it is a brilliant array of poetry and subject matter. The selector's and poet's commentary make for intriguing reading, I really hope they inspire you to either try a new poet's work or invest in the latest from one already known to you.

We're delighted to announce the winners of our Metro Poetry Prize too, Nicola Sealey and D.A. Prince. The prize was run in partnership with Nexus and judged by Alice at the PBS and the poet Degna Stone to give a platform to poetry in our local community. You can read the first prize-winning poem at the back of the *Bulletin* or see them printed on giant poster boards at Longbenton Metro Station in Tyne and Wear.

We'd also like to thank Mary Jean Chan for her excellent pamphlet selections over the last year, this is her final selection for the PBS and she hands over the baton to Nina Mingya Powles in the summer. We can't wait to share her selections.

SOPHIE O'NEILL
PBS & INPRESS DIRECTOR

EMILY BERRY

Emily Berry is the author of three poetry books: *Dear Boy* (2013), *Stranger, Baby* (2017) and *Unexhausted Time* (2022). She writes *sleepcasts* (bedtime stories) for the meditation app Headspace, and was a co-writer of *The Breakfast Bible* (2013), a compendium of breakfasts. Her lyric essay on agoraphobia, dreams and the imagination, 'The Secret Country of Her Mind', appears in the artist's book *Many Nights* (2021) by Jacqui Kenny. She is a fellow of the Royal Society of Literature and editor of *The Poetry Review*, and lives in London, where she was born.

UNEXHAUSTED TIME

FABER | £10.99 | PBS PRICE £8.25

Emily Berry
Unexhausted
Time

In Emily Berry's third full-length collection, *Unexhausted Time*, an astute shift in tone and theatre raises the book into an atmosphere of weighty searching, restlessness, and surprise. Berry is a master at prudently organising pronouns to complicate narratives and speakers – a feature she's widely celebrated for in both her previous collections. The opening sequence balances a tension between speaker and addressee, one that resists clarity yet manages to beguile the reader by building enough trust, enabling poems to maintain their sense of delight and intrigue.

> I decided to try and write to you
> about what I'm experiencing, since
> I have no techniques for helping myself.

The language gestures and bends into more obscure subjects, cultivating an asocial or timeless vortex which tugs the lens closer towards the speaker. The focus and psychology of the work appears in part to be retroactive, "It was a nice house, quite plain and tasteful, but it had a bad atmosphere. I don't like the way things have turned out, but the law is the law." Moving rapidly from a state of remembering into the present, Berry disrupts the very function of time through the foundation of memory, political malaise, and place.

One is never quite able to lose the sense of frustration and indignation in the collection's overall character. Poems appear to be in conversation with each other or resisting each other, adding more layers to the book's remit. Inflections of high Modernist writing, essayism and philosophical candour give rise to the political castigation which subtly tints much of the book. In 'Nocturne' a distinction is drawn between hypocritical conduct at a state level and how time / history very often repeats:

> I never
> saw the birth of a moon, but I witnessed
> many beheadings, in our country this is
> usual. I never saw a head that did not grow
> back, sometimes bigger than before.

Unexhausted Time is as majestic as it is impressive, destabilizing inner and outer worlds through an extraordinary dialectic.

ANTHONY ANAXAGOROU

SELECTOR'S COMMENT

EMILY BERRY

I recently read an article by the writer Lucie Elven in *The New York Times* about "time slips", anecdotal experiences of time travel in which individuals claim to have caught a glimpse of a former (or future) time in the present. This has never happened to me, but I believe in it; I mean, I believe it is a true representation of how little we (in the West, at least) actually comprehend the relationship between past, present and future.

Unexhausted Time probably began when I became obsessed with a quote from Anne Carson's *Economy of the Unlost*, which provides my book's title and epigraph: " 'Attempts at description are stupid', George Eliot says, yet one may encounter a fragment of unexhausted time. Who can name its transactions, the sense that fell through us of untouchable wind, unknown effort – one black mane?" A fragment of unexhausted time could be another way of describing a time slip, those things that return to us as unfinished business, which we might also call memories, but they are world-memories, not just personal ones.

I traced Carson's quote back to its source in Eliot's *Daniel Deronda*: "Attempts at description are stupid: who can all at once describe a human being? Even when he is presented to us we only begin that knowledge of his appearance which must be completed by innumerable impressions under differing circumstances. We recognise the alphabet; we are not sure of the language."

Unexhausted Time seems to take up this challenge: attempting to name these transactions, to describe a human being – or, shall we say, life – all at once.

EMILY RECOMMENDS ─────────────

Inger Christensen, trans. Susanna Nied, *alphabet* (Bloodaxe); CA Conrad, *The Book of Frank* (Wave); Athena Farrokhzad, trans. Jennifer Hayashida, *White Blight* (Argos Books); Ross Gay, *Catalog of Unabashed Gratitude* (Pitt Poetry Series); Itō Hiromi, trans. Jeffrey Angles, *Killing Kanoko / Wild Grass on the Riverbank* (Tilted Axis); Christine Marendon, trans. Ken Cockburn, *Heroines from Abroad* (Carcanet); Kathryn Maris, *The House with Only an Attic and a Basement* (Penguin); Mary Ruefle, *Trances of the Blast* (Wave); *The Horse Has Six Legs: Contemporary Serbian Poetry*, trans. Charles Simic (Graywolf).

I CHOICE

UNEXHAUSTED TIME

For a number of months I had observed
astonishing quantities of rain. Spring rain,
summer rain, autumn rain. *The sound of
heavy winter rain.* It was a strange time
and I loved to go to sleep, I loved to go
to the top of the hill in the pale light
of dawn and think back to the world
I knew. *Small fragments of war suspended
in everyday life.* An unfathomable cessation
of industry. On our street there were
saplings supported by stakes so they would
not lean, yet some, nonetheless, leaned.
Everyone was small and touched with light.
*I took the measure of the unbearable vanity
of the West, that has never ceased to privilege being
over non-being, what is spoken to what is unsaid.*
A feeling was named and I was sorry then
to have lost its magic unknownness,
the way it would come to mind like a
remembered secret and then slip away...
One day my therapist told me we were finished,
our sessions could come to an end. I protested
that I wasn't ready, I still needed more help,
please, I begged her, but she was insistent
and even radiant with the news. I was cured
and I would not need to come again.

I felt I was born in a time when a lot of stuff
was just... not known... So we asked,
what was it like, to be a human being...?
The clouds flushed with their
ridiculous secret, light.
Our minds like a playing field in spring...
Most feelings are very old, they have
been under the earth and then up
to the surface again, they have been
in the vapour of clouds and all across
the surface of the sky like hairline cracks
in the glaze on porcelain, our motivations
under the river like pebbles or like the lives
of unseen creatures that keep us alive...
There was a song we had never heard before,
it was a very old song, it was a song
we once knew but an imaginary one.
Listening to it was like looking at the sky
at a certain time of day, on certain days,
in midsummer, as it slowly pulls itself apart.
There were so many times I wanted to give up
but then a message would appear
from a complete stranger, from miles away,
telling me to go on. So I went on.

WILL ALEXANDER

Will Alexander is a critically acclaimed, LA-based poet, philosopher and visual artist. He has won a Whiting Fellowship for Poetry, a California Arts Council Fellowship, and a 2016 Jackson Poetry Prize. He has published numerous collections with various publishers in the US. *Refractive Africa* will be his first UK publication.

REFRACTIVE AFRICA

GRANTA | £10.99 | PBS PRICE £8.25

Will Alexander is a poet of classical higher thought, linguistic dexterity, epistemology, and attentiveness. In *Refractive Africa* he unravels an intellectual labyrinth, sustaining the kind of virtuosic energy you might expect to find if Ludwig Wittgenstein and Charlie Parker sat down to collaborate on a poem. There is nothing simple or straightforward about the way Alexander approaches his preoccupations; an honest reflection of the complications contained within themes of colonialism, Pan-Africanism, the diasporic experience, the occult and ancient histories. It's at once a lesson and an immersive experience in how poetry can be used as an instrument to both edify and excite the senses.

Refractive Africa is a collection comprised of three major meditations, each dealing with a specific strand of European colonial capitalism, and the subsequent impact it's had on the African continent. With critical gestures towards those nations who forcefully enslaved, exploited, and displaced Africans, Alexander prefaces the book with "what I attempt to unleash in *Refractive Africa* is an organic emboldening of the African psyche, a postcolonial inner power that allows this poetic text to electrify an energy that the Occident continues to distort."

Working out from the theories and arguments posited by distinguished 20th century scholars such as Cheikh Anta Diop, C.L.R. James and Cedric Robinson, *Refractive Africa* is simultaneously a reckoning with history as well as an indictment of European thought and behaviour:

> this harassment
> this pastiche of Belgian instigation
> aligned to psychic displacement
> as criminal disparagement
> always directed towards strife
> towards a lagoon infected by caimans & fatigue

Refractive Africa is a boundless reclaiming of both personal and historic narrative; it's a challenge, a force. A poetic which demands as much attention as the pained and knotted subjects it artfully inhabits.

ANTHONY ANAXAGOROU

WILL ALEXANDER

My inspiration for *Refractive Africa* remains a non-didactic, internal verbal eruption. Not a verbal eruption restricted to topical events but concerned with the continent. A protracted historical struggle as it has occurred, not only within the palpable recollection of our prior century, but of Africa perceived as a historical deficit to be exploited. The latter stretches back to initial Portuguese entry into Africa in the 14th century.

This book not only concerns itself with palpable events germane to recent memory but also with the psychological wreckage that has accrued over time. The triumvirate of poems in this work spontaneously indicates a state of living psychological royalty pressured by existential duress that has attacked the African mind via both palpable and impalpable hostilities.

In this sense *Refractive Africa: Ballet of the Forgotten* is a homage to a continent endowed with an almost mystical character as it has survived both overt and covert hostilities having risen above the maze that continues to attempt at methods that provoke its almost seismic assassination.

This stanza seems to sum up the extenuating charity that remains the Congo:

> thus
>
> duplicitous tragedy
> innate with micro-centric suffering
> its stressful indictment
> its tertiary wounding
> its camps its darkened glossolalia
> at the height of bloody moonrise

WILL RECOMMENDS

Anthony Seidman, *The Defining Crisis of Your Lifetime is Utopia* (Trainwreck Press); Adam Cornford, *Lalia* (Chax Press); Giorgia Pavlidou, *Inside the black hornets mind-tunnel* (Trainwreck Press); Tongo Eisen-Martin, *Heaven is All Goodbyes* (City Lights); Heller Levinson, *Wrack Lariat* (Black Widow Press); Nathaniel Mackey, *Splay Anthem* (New Directions); Marcela Durand, *Area* (Belladonna); Andrew Joron, *The Sound Mirror* (Flood Editions); Garrett Caples, *Lovers of Today* (Wave Books); Ariel Resnikoff, *Unnatural Bird Migrator* (The Operating System); Carlos Lara, *Like Bismuth When I Enter* (Nightboat Books).

I RECOMMENDATION

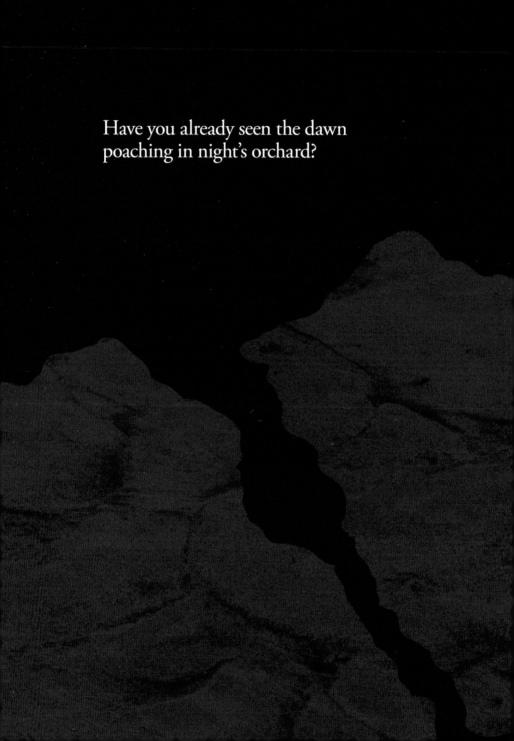

Have you already seen the dawn
poaching in night's orchard?

THE CONGO (AN EXTRACT)

As Akashic sangoma*
I peer into the Congo
as transpersonal witness
as incisively faceted tiger
squirming
having the powers of a shark
via forces that sculpt the lenticular as lightning
perhaps a telepathic wakefulness
perhaps magisterial conjuration
creating migrational litmus in my blood
thereby knowing the dangerous template that is the Congo

blood infected
dazed conundrum
horrific with grandeur
solemnly lit by grainy episodes of lightning

thus
duplicitous tragedy
innate with micro-centric suffering
its stressful indictment
its tertiary woundings
its camps its darkened glossolalia
at the height of bloody moonrise

*Akashic sangoma: Psychophysical healer of West African origin.

FIONA BENSON

Fiona Benson won the Forward Prize for Best Collection 2019 for *Vertigo & Ghost* (Cape). Her first collection *Bright Travellers* (Cape, 2014) won the 2015 Seamus Heaney Centre Prize for a First Full Collection and the 2015 Geoffrey Faber Memorial Prize. She lives in Devon with her husband and their two daughters.

EPHEMERON

CAPE | £12.00 | PBS PRICE £9.00

Ephemeron follows hot on the heels of Benson's Forward Prize-winning 2019 collection, *Vertigo & Ghost*. It continues that book's re-encountering of Greek myth as a way of making poems that speak to very contemporary concerns. Where the Zeus sequence of *Vertigo & Ghost* offered a way of thinking about male sexual violence in the wake of #MeToo, the long central section of this new book, 'Translations from the Pasiphaë', turns its lens on female desire. Benson centres this extraordinary sequence on Pasiphaë, the mother of the Minotaur, known primarily in Greek myth for the bestial sexual hunger that saw her couple with a bull, birthing the monster imprisoned in the labyrinth:

> But I wanted a child
> and must eat. At first, a mouthful here and there,
> but then my body asserted itself, I could've devoured
> a feast for ten and still come back for more.

But what makes these poems so powerful in the end, so moving as well as unsettling, is the way Benson fleshes out Pasiphaë as a mother to a child born "different":

> He was beautiful, my son.
> In his sleep, he shone.
> I kissed the wet tufts of his fur,
> his damp snout

This intimate portrait of Pasiphaë's motherly love radically challenges the focus of the traditional myth, with its valorisation of the monster-slaying hero Theseus.

The story of the labyrinth echoes elsewhere in the book: in its first part, 'Insect Love Songs', cicadas emerge from their subterranean realm ("Little solitaries / excavating chambers / deep underground, / daubed cells"), while a mother cockroach is "joyfully promiscuous". Another stand-out section, offering yet another variation on Pasiphaë's "hunger", is 'Boarding-School Tales', which evokes the pent-up sexuality of teenage girls on the cusp of adulthood:

> our virginity shining like the pristine white tips
> of a new pair of Converse
> demanding to be scuffed.

SARAH HOWE

FIONA BENSON

Ephemeron is a book of four parts, with overarching themes of desire, imprisonment, and motherhood. The first part, 'Insect Love Songs' is the fruit of a commission from Arts & Culture at the University of Exeter, who generously funded my research into the brief and urgent lives of insects. With radio producers Mair Bosworth and Eliza Lomas I travelled from the back lanes of my own village, where a colony of glow worms studs the hedgerow, to the Smoky Mountains, where I witnessed the display of synchronous fireflies, interviewing scores of scientists along the way. Much of what I learned felt relatable and familiar; much seemed extraordinary, bizarre, and unknowable.

I was particularly intrigued by the way in which insects rear or do not rear their offspring – indeed, there is a poem in praise of the good mothering practices of cockroaches – and I think being a mother has cast me back on my own childhood in sometimes uncomfortable ways. We were an RAF family who moved location at least eight times before I reached the age of eleven. At eleven my sister and I were sent to boarding school and, like most Forces kids, thereby occupy a strange place of disrupted childhoods and privilege / not privilege. 'Boarding School Tales' explores some of the hauntings I still carry from that time.

The third section 'Translations from the Pasiphaë' retells the story of Pasiphaë and the birth and life of the minotaur. It reimagines the minotaur as a disabled child. Ancient Greek convention was to expose disabled children. I imagine instead that the healer Pasiphaë (sister to that other famous healer and witch, Circe) chose to keep her son. I try and recentralise Pasiphaë as the powerful Queen at the heart of so many Greek myths, rather than as a culturally debased figure, the woman who slept with a bull; and I explore her husband King Minos' descent into brutality and slaughter. Lastly, 'Daughter Mother' explores the tender underside of motherhood – its failures and anxieties, as well as its savage love.

FIONA RECOMMENDS

Hannah Hodgson, *Where I'd Watch Plastic Trees Not Grow* (Verve) and *163 Days* (Seren); Sunnah Khan, *I Don't Know How to Forgive You When You Make No Apology for this Haunting* and *The 4 Brown Girls Who Write Collective* (Rough Trade Books); Katie Byford, *He Said I Was A Peach* (Ignitionpress); Charlotte Knight, *Ways of Healing* (smith/doorstop); Kim Moore, *All the Men I Never Married* (Seren). Anything ever by Liz Berry, Jay Bernard, Malika Booker, Séan Hewitt, Wayne Holloway-Smith, Amaan Hyder, Andrew McMillan, Robin Robertson, Richard Scott, Danez Smith, Matthew Dickman, Sharon Olds. Watch out for ferocious rising stars, Remi Graves and Dianty Ningrum.

Will we ever find our way back home?

PASIPHAË ON ASTERIOS' DEATH

I had not thought he would survive;
the day he said "ma", I cried.

My last-born son, who always wanted
to be tickled, who luxuriated in touch,

who'd lie his heavy head in my lap
to be stroked, and sing his thanks.

Who, even in his confusion,
shone with love – for me, for Ariadne,

for his brothers and sisters in the palace.
Who, when I cried, pressed his cheek against mine.

The son I thought I would have by my side
till I myself was dead.

Minos thought he was a curse.
In fact, he was the greatest gift.

They took him away from me
and they killed him in the dark, for years.

WARSAN SHIRE

Warsan Shire is a Somali-British writer and poet born in Nairobi and raised in London. She has written two chapbooks, *Teaching My Mother How To Give Birth* and *Her Blue Body*, and is included in the Penguin Modern Poets series. She was awarded the inaugural Brunel International African Poetry Prize and served as the first Young Poet Laureate of London. Warsan wrote the poetry for the Peabody Award-winning visual album *Lemonade* and Disney film *Black Is King* in collaboration with Beyoncé Knowles-Carter. She lives in Los Angeles with her husband and two children. *Bless the Daughter Raised by a Voice in Her Head* is her first full collection.

BLESS THE DAUGHTER...

CHATTO & WINDUS | £12.99 | PBS PRICE £9.75

WARSAN SHIRE

BLESS THE DAUGHTER
RAISED BY A VOICE
IN HER HEAD

It seems extraordinary that Warsan Shire has not published a first full collection of poems till now, such has been the impact of her two pamphlets, *Teaching My Mother How to Give Birth* and *Her Blue Body*. Poems from the former inspired and ran through Beyoncé's visual album, *Lemonade*, catapulting Shire to a degree of fame more usually associated with pop icons. This collection's release will thrill a devoted fanbase, online and otherwise. There is an aphoristic resonance to her writing that means certain lines and passages lend themselves to circulating, meme-like, on social media, as if passed from hand to hand: "No one leaves home unless home is the mouth of a shark" and:

> My alone feels so good,
> I'll only have you if you're sweeter
> than my solitude.

This book performs the task of gathering the existing poems and placing them in new contexts and arrangements, set off by a proportion of previously unseen work. There is a strangeness to encountering old favourites reworked: I'm not sure I can get used to 'The House' shorn of its numbered section breaks, for example.

When the phrase from the book's title appears in situ within a poem, the "voices" in the head become plural:

> Mama, I made it
> out of your home
> alive, raised by
> the voices
> in my head

Shire's poetic voice has always had this sense of being choral, of channelling a community of voices on African diaspora and womanhood, on refugee experience, through its singular, lyric "I". Here the voices take on an uncanny aspect: the "burden of representation" as a sort of haunting, perhaps. The artful line breaks help to activate the double meaning of "made it / out of" ("escaped from", but also "created it from") – a pun that sums up the way survival and creation exist side-by-side in Shire's searing, original work.

WARSAN SHIRE

When Britney Spears said "My loneliness is killing me", I had always applied this to the untethered, overwhelming loneliness experienced by family. I grew up surrounded by grief, it took up all the space, all the time.

"Writing saved me from the sin and the inconvenience of violence." – Alice Walker

An uncle once described his dreams as "buildings to be destroyed in the morning" and so this casual poetry, this easy lament – created a small opening for the steam to release. The alternative was unmentionable.

Poetry was passed on to me, a supreme gift. This is an ode to my unhinged women and their distraught, melancholic men. This is a celebration of their wicked humour and bewildering strength, their courage and bombastic love.

I return to the mother wound often, I am trying to understand my fleshy roots. This book is an exploration of my girlhood and its many rituals. How far do the tentacles of childhood reach? A study on the emotional and psychological repercussions of war and trauma. It is a kiss through time, a benediction for the parentified child. A rite of passage, an examination of family and memory. A love letter to my child self.

WARSAN RECOMMENDS

Pascale Petit, *The Zoo Father* (Seren); Roger Robinson, *Suitcase* (Flipped Eye); Terrance Hayes, *Lighthead* (Penguin); A. Van Jordan, *Macnolia* (Norton); Ai, *Cruelty* (Houghton Mifflin Harcourt Publishing); Malika Booker, *Pepper Seed* (Peepal Tree Press); Karen McCarthy Woolf, *An Aviary of Small Birds* (Carcanet); Patricia Smith, *Incendiary Art* (Bloodaxe Books); Jacob Sam La-Rose, *Breaking Silence* (Bloodaxe Books); Kayo Chingonyi, *Kumukanda* (Chatto); Jay Bernard, *Surge* (Chatto); Inua Ellams, *The Actual* (Nine Arches Press); Ross Gay, *Catalog of Unabashed Gratitude* (Pitt Poetry); Hiromi Itō, *Killing Kanoko* (Tilted Axis); Bernardine Evaristo, *Girl, Woman, Other* (Penguin); Kwame Dawes, *City of Bones* (Peepal Tree).

Your daughter's face is a small ric
her hands are a civil war,

FILIAL CANNIBALISM

From time to time
mothers in the wild
devour their young,
an appetite born of
pure, bright need.
Occasionally,
mothers from ordinary
homes, much like our
own, feed on the viscid
shame their daughters
are forced to secrete
from glands formed
in the favour of men.

WARSAN SHIRE

Image: Brid O'Donovan

JESSICA TRAYNOR

Jessica Traynor was born in Dublin in 1984 and is a poet, essayist and librettist. Her debut collection, *Liffey Swim* (Dedalus Press, 2014), was shortlisted for the Strong/Shine Award and in 2016 was named one of the best poetry debuts of the past five years on Bustle. com. In 2016, she was also named one of the "Rising Generation" of poets by Poetry Ireland. Her second collection, *The Quick*, was a 2019 *Irish Times* poetry choice. *Pit Lullabies* (Bloodaxe Books, 2022) is her third collection. She reviews poetry for RTÉ's Arena, and for *Poetry Ireland Review*, and has held residencies including at the Yeats Society, Sligo, and Carlow College. She is an inaugural Creative Fellow of UCD, where she completed her MA in Creative Writing in 2008, and is Dún Laoghaire-Rathdown Writer in Residence for 2021-22.

PIT LULLABIES
BLOODAXE | £10.99 | PBS PRICE £8.25

Here an acerbic wit is fused with ruminations on the female body along with the concerns of early parenthood. These motifs inform major parts of Jessica Traynor's third collection, *Pit Lullabies*. The interiority of a new mother's mind is, over the course of the book, infatuated or fraught, cautious or uncertain. The poems which launch the collection travel through linear time to trace the experiences of a mother in the early stages of pregnancy. As the poems progress, allusions towards the complications of childbirth, and the threat it poses to both the female body and mind are excavated and intensified.

Poems appear anchored to specific locales; from scanning and birthing rooms through to kitchens, parks, or a wintery day. Traynor manages to embrace the amazement and joy of parenthood, along with its more foreboding counterpart. The poems centre not only on the needs of a newborn, but those of a parent, as suggested in the final stanza of 'Ophelia in Ballybough':

> Our filaments reknit in their own crooked way.
> I wheel the baby home. The days darken
> into winter, lose their odd electric gleam,
> the moon skips back into her orbit.

The stark bifurcation of a world in motion, while at home a mother watches "the baby's wiggle" or "her liquid grin" adds a genuine tenderness to the work. In 'What It Takes', the speaker subverts Judeo-Christian ideas of maternity to focus on the stamina and diligence required to physically give birth. In 'On Poisons' the book changes tone, calling on the more dangerous aspects of human life which taunt a parent's mind.

> Find a wood and set your child loose
> to forage flowers and berries.
> Warn them to steer clear of nettles,
> of men who travel alone, or in packs.

Traynor's sound is effortlessly hypnotic, her language formed, deliberate and lyrical.

ANTHONY ANAXAGOROU

SELECTOR'S COMMENT

JESSICA TRAYNOR

In 2019, while working as a judge for Ireland's national theatre awards, I made many journeys by night. My daughter was young at the time and I'd find myself standing after midnight at bus stops in distant cities and towns, waiting for a bus that would bring me home to her.

I was reading Gaston Bachelard's *The Poetics of Space*, with its idea of the cellar: "the dark entity of the house, the one that partakes of subterranean forces." There are times in our lives when we find ourselves in these spaces, and for me it was a place I'd been consigned to by motherhood. In the act of becoming a parent I felt like a layer of skin had been permanently flayed from me, and the demands of my work-life – constantly pulling me away from my child – were exacerbating that vulnerability. I was always far away, and it was always dark.

In writing about motherhood, I wasn't interested in evoking the easy warmth that exists between mother and child; my experience was more complicated than that. Instead, I tried to interrogate the acute angles of experience, the anxieties that plagued me. So while travelling, I wrote a series of messages to my daughter, fragments of poems that tried to capture the fractured dream-space in which I found myself. They were most often warnings; about poisons, and violence, and extinction, all sent from the Night Gates of various bus terminals and train stations.

Bachelard goes on to say of the cellar, "When we dream there, we are in harmony with the irrationality of the depths." *Pit Lullabies* is an attempt to pull those irrationalities out of the dark for my daughter, pin them squirming on paper for her to see.

JESSICA RECOMMENDS

Dean Browne, *Kitchens at Night* (Poetry Business); Rosamund Taylor, *In Her Jaws* (Banshee Press); Jess McKinney, *Weeding* (Hazel Press); Elaine Feeney, *Rise* (Salmon); Annemarie Ní Churreáin, *The Poison Glen* (The Gallery Press); Adam Wyeth, *about:blank* (Salmon); Gail McConnell, *The Sun is Open* (Penned in the Margins); Nidhi Zak/Aria Eipe, *Auguries of a Minor God* (Faber); Katie Forde, *Blood Lyrics* (Graywolf); David Keplinger, *The World to Come* (Conduit Books); Emily Cooper, *Glass* (Makina Books).

RECOMMENDATION

Learn to turn regret into pity
for the limbs you never owned.

Image: Jean Léon Gérôme

PIT LULLABY

A whisper in your ear as you sleep –
when I was carrying you,
and you were an electrical storm,
a clump of eels behind the gut,
I cursed a man.

I called all of my demons down
from their rookeries to carry your shock
of legs and stingers to latch onto him.
He thrashed till the whole writhing mess
sank back into a bog pool,
silted, silent.

We witches aren't world-beaters my darling,
we're a needle through the thimble,
the gape of a paper-cut,
mild misfortune
whose sorrow
is always
absorbed.

DENISE RILEY

Denise Riley is a critically acclaimed writer of both philosophy and poetry. She is currently Professor of the History of Ideas and of Poetry at UEA. Her visiting positions have included A.D. White Professor at Cornell University in the US, Writer in Residence at the Tate Gallery in London, and Visiting Fellow at Birkbeck College in the University of London. She has taught philosophy, art history, poetics, and creative writing. Denise Riley lives in London.

LUREX

PICADOR | £10.99 | PBS PRICE £8.25

After the long silence that led up to the publication of *Say Something Back* in 2016, a new collection from Riley feels like a significant event. In the meantime, Picador has published a revised *Selected Poems* (2019), designed to make accessible to a wider readership the arc of her singular poetics across years of publishing with small and experimental presses. There is the sense in *Lurex* of a poet recoiling from this greater degree of (self-)exposure:

> Hush, jeremiads, flat as milk
> where not bubbling under the blood.
> And I myself in cramoisie.

So begins the collection's title poem, with its ambivalent embarkation from silence into speech. The speaker shushes the personified "jeremiads" (long complaints or lamentations) like fractious children. She has dressed herself in "cramoisie", an archaic term for crimson-coloured cloth – like a scarlet woman making a spectacle of herself through verse? The poem's quicksilver tonal shifts ("Dark yet sparkly – / the seriousness of it!") speak to the titular Lurex, whose sparkle is artificial, dated, gaudy, gendered – I can't help hearing "lurid" behind it. Can something "sparkly" be serious?

The collection continues Riley's career-long interrogation of and quarrel with "identity", gendered and otherwise. To this end, several of its lyric shards reprise what Sam Solomon has called Riley's "serious play with personal pronouns":

> To write the word she does less than you might think. Or it does more.
> To write the word she does more than you might want. Or it does less.

The search for an unmarked, neutral pronoun is upturned, devastatingly, in '1948' when we learn how the speaker "stayed in it" in the abusive adoptive household where she was raised an orphan, next to the "real beloved dog I envied". That stunning long poem is the book's heart and its wound, self-consciously reluctant about its swerve into confession: "She's damaged. TMI?"

LUREX

Hush, jeremiads, flat as milk
where not bubbling under the blood.
And I myself in cramoisie.

The fathers look to their veins.
The blood has it. Could they not have
trusted in themselves, and so in us.

Not easy in their leaving:
"How do I know it's mine?"
How am I mine, who once was yours.

Dark yet sparkly –
the seriousness of it!
To believe in both its *then* and its *now*.

A child as a guarantor
against loneliness, including its own:
one fact that is kinder all round.

WONG MAY

Wong May was born in Chongqing, China, grew up in Singapore and has lived in Dublin since the 1970s. Wong May received her Bachelor of Arts degree in English Literature, from the University of Singapore and a Master of Fine Arts from the University of Iowa. Her fourth book of poems *Picasso's Tears* included work from 1978–2013 and was published by Octopus Books in 2014.

IN THE SAME LIGHT: 200 TANG POEMS FOR OUR CENTURY

CARCANET | £19.99 | PBS   PRICE   £15.00

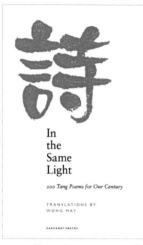

Tang poetry is one of the world's great storehouses of language and thought, a centuries-long period in which poetry was woven through both popular and political culture. Wong May's selection and translation thinks this poetry through dispossession, migration and exile, the task less a question of making Tang relevant to our century and more a persistent tugging on the common threads of feeling that are readily available in the original. The result is a book very contemporary in its human closeness.

Brevity of phrasing and generous lineation reveal the work. Where archaism or fussy grammar might have frozen the verse, a light touch and an open page allow the poetry to flow with clarity, offering a connection to the source. The period's clichés are of the melancholy poet alone in nature, but here, as in Du Fu's well-known 'Spring View', poet and nature are set in their political context:

> The country has fallen.
>
> Mountains & rivers
> Remain.
>
> Spring comes to the city.

Across the book, the poetry works through upheaval, through movement and stillness, willed and unwilled. Wong May offers an extensive Afterword on the poetry and its interpreters. No mere translator's note, this capacious essay is historical, critical, comical, personal, structural and mystical by turns, exploring the Tang context of the original poets and the poetry's echoes over the last millennium or so, up through Pound and Mao to *The Dharma Bums*. Wong May hopes "to return the text to the body of world literature" through her investigations as a translator and critic. Her work deserves this hope, which is better than any reparative aim for poetry, always complicit in and resistant to the politics of its times. As Meng Jiao writes through Wong May (or vice versa):

> Bad poetry gets you good posts.
> Good poetry
> Gets you to a mountain.

SPRING VIEW

The country has fallen.

Mountains & rivers
Remain.

Spring comes to the city.
            The woods deepen.
Grass grows into thickets.

Hard times

            Flowers are seen in tears,

Fresh off parting,
A bird's cry is
Terror to hear.

Beacon fires
Continuous
        For three months

                "A letter from home is
Worth
        Taels of gold"?

                    I raked my grizzled head,
                    Hard times
                    Short on hair
                                Little there
                    To hold a hat pin.

Written in captivity by Du Fu, Chang'an, 757

PIP OSMOND-WILLIAMS

Pip Osmond-Williams is a poet, editorial assistant and academic researcher from the north of England living in Glasgow. Her writing draws on nature and mythology to reflect on grief, love and other aspects of human connection. Her poems have appeared in *Poetry Scotland, Gutter, Channel,* and *New Writing Scotland,* among others. In 2021, she won the Brian Dempsey Memorial Competition for her debut pamphlet *Of Algae & Grief.*

OF ALGAE & GRIEF

DEMPSEY & WINDLE | £8.00 |

I have spent some time with this collection by Pip Osmond-Williams. The work is ambitious. I get the sense that the poet is testing language beyond its limits. Language could also be a proxy for the world, life, and emotion. The experiment begins with the first poem when the poet observes.

> you say I can't keep doing this
>   that somebody found me
> trying to swim with the mute swans again
>   telling them about the scythe-winged swifts
>   & bone-pin whitethroats

The next obvious question then is why is the poet putting the world/life/emotion/language under such scrutiny? My instinct tells me that one plausible reason is that the poet is consumed by the desire to understand the body. When I say body, we are not limited by the human body and its cognisance. One should also consider bodies of water, the body of a bird, the body of the earth. It is through the body that we perceive the world or as Leonardo da Vinci said "All our knowledge has its origins in our perceptions". Observe Osmond-Williams incite on the body:

> Sometimes the body is just cavity
> to crawl between, moor beneath,
> hands stretched out to bronchi of myth and fog.

This musing on different spectrums of the body is a rational way to deal with the more intimate natures of the collection which are loss and grief. Notice how loss and grief are measured in a temporal way.

> Air gathers in a cotton well
> upon my tongue. Time's unstitched from
> my throat their names you knew, but they
> live in my body like a harp

We are capturing Osmond-Williams' thoughts and emotions in all these lines. We heard in succession how they act like musical movements. That is my roundabout way of saying each line and each poem is well composed.

GIRLSONG

you say I can't keep doing this

                             that somebody found me

trying to swim with the mute swans again

                telling them about the scythe-winged swifts

                    & bone-pin whitethroats

how the migratory birds outfly me when I call

                         you say that in the water

somebody found me measuring the lengths

of all I love in knots   of sweet galingale

that when the wardens came

my arms & hands were cottongrass &

            from the side it looked as though my mouth

                    was speckled blue & O

a song thrush egg or a scream

       through which I try to heave the lilies from my throat

& somehow come up empty

            you say that when they finally slipped me

from my raincoat & freshwater hoops

of algae & grief

               I kept talking about monotypic species

     about white rings pooled around Lir

about how I must call my mother

JEREMY HOOKER

Jeremy Hooker was born in 1941 and grew up in Warsash near Southampton, and the landscape of this region has remained an important source of inspiration. Many of his poems were written in Wales, where he has lived for long periods of his life, and now lives in retirement. His academic career took him to universities in the Netherlands and the USA and he was Professor of English at the University of Glamorgan before his retirement. Alongside his many collections of poetry, including a *Collected Poems* from Enitharmon and a *Selected Poems 1965–2018* from Shearsman Books, Hooker is also well-known as a critic and has published selections of writings by Edward Thomas and Richard Jefferies, as well as studies of David Jones and John Cowper Powys, all of them important to his own creative life.

THE RELEASE

SHEARSMAN | £10.95 | PBS PRICE £8.22

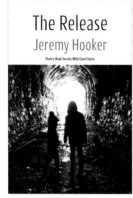

The Release

Jeremy Hooker

Poetry Book Society Wild Card Choice

Since *Welsh Journal* (2001), I have periodically adopted a form of writing that juxtaposes prose and poetry. *The Release* is a work of this kind, in which diary entries and poems are combined and interact. Roughly speaking, the diary records experience that generates the poems, or, to use another metaphor, the poems disclose their roots in the prose.

Between June 2019 and August 2020, I spent four long periods in hospital, initially in Prince Charles Hospital in Merthyr Tydfil, and latterly in the Renal Unit at The Heath in Cardiff. The diary records my experience as a patient and reflects aspects of the life of the hospital; the poems respond to what I felt and saw in the ward, but also go beyond being a record of everyday reality. Like my *Diary of a Stroke* and other journals, *The Release* is a poet's journal. In ways that the book describes, the periods of hospitalization proved to be intensely creative. This was partly due to having so much time to write and read and think, together with the ever-present sense of mortality. Long days and some sleepless nights in bed were conducive to memory, and stimulated me to write, as well as the poems, rough drafts of two books: *Addiction*: a love story, and a memoir of my life in Wales. These are, as it were, backgrounds to the material of which *The Release* is composed.

In editing the material, I have focused mainly on two things: the reality of days and nights confined to a hospital bed, and the life of the mind, intellectual and spiritual, which finds expression in poetry. At times, in the process of writing poems, or drafts of poems, I was acutely aware of the workings of the imagination, and of feeling my way to a better understanding of poetry as a magnetic "field of force". As I wrote in the diary, I realized that: "A stream of thinking and feeling, a lyrical stream, has been released in my mind". This is partly what *The Release* is about, and I have edited the diary with this theme in mind. But this is not only a book concerned with poetry, or with self-reflection. It is also a tribute to the modern hospital as a place of care and healing. In Prince Charles Hospital and at The Heath, I experienced "the reality of democracy" that characterises our National Health Service. This was all the more impressive in contrast to the noise of the outer, political world, and in view of the pressures on staff due to the Covid virus.

ARCHIE

Archie, great-
grandson, welcome
to a world that will be
for you, I pray, a place
to breathe in, free
of pestilence, and not
mired by human filth.

You will not know me,
Archie, unless in a poem
but may imagine me,
if you care to, thinking
of you, little boy in a bobble hat,
joy of your parents, delight
of all your kin.
        Soon, you will be ready
to set out, adventuring,
pushing aside old stories,
as you make your way
finding new words for a world
where, I trust, fresh winds will blow.

SPRING BOOK REVIEWS

MONIZA ALVI: FAIROZ
REVIEWED BY PRAYTUSHA

Moniza Alvi's latest collection *Fairoz* lingers, meditatively at times, on what it means to feel isolated from country, religion, and family. Alvi sensitively excavates the loneliness of a figurative girlhood, writing, "she's edging out of one story, / looking both ways. Not looking. / She hasn't left – but she has gone". The narrative structure, like the fragments of ice that Alvi writes about, draws out the questions and fears of imaginary Fairoz in vignettes.

MARCH | BLOODAXE | £10.99 | PBS PRICE £8.25

DIANA ANPHIMIADI: WHY I NO LONGER WRITE POEMS
REVIEWED BY SHALINI SENGUPTA

Collaboratively translated by Jean Sprackland and Natalia Bukia-Peters, *Why I No Longer Write Poems* captures the intricate imagination of Diana Anphimiadi as it glides through classical allusions and surrealist imagery. Several poems oscillate between decay and regeneration; hope and despair. They turn on the notion of love: distilled into a "snapshot" that buoys the creative energies, and dilates the boundaries, of the poetic form. Together, they bear testament to the formal range and breadth of Anphimiadi's writing.

FEB | BLOODAXE | £12.99 | PBS PRICE £9.75

KWAME DAWES AND JOHN KINSELLA: UNHISTORY
REVIEWED BY SHALINI SENGUPTA

Dawes and Kinsella present an intense exploration of history and its relationship with poetry. Each poem unravels the tightly wrought cords of "history": reframing it variously as mourning; amnesia; and hope. Boldly inventive, they tug at a range of references: drawn from biblical as well as historical sources, lived experience and the unspoken everyday. "Life is history," Dawes and Kinsella conclude, offering a glimpse of the eternal in their poetic bricolage.

MARCH | PEEPAL TREE PRESS | £19.99 | PBS PRICE £15

LEDBURY CRITICS TAKEOVER

Amali Gunasekera's second collection is a beautiful examination of the separateness and union of "I" and "You", rooted in an English pastoral tradition reminiscent of Wordsworth and the Lake Poets. Myth, the natural world, the ephemeral beauty of music or the filter of light on a wintry morning, unite to articulate love for the "Beloved". These are masterful poems of intimacy and joy leading to places of stillness and wisdom.

MARCH | BLOODAXE | £10.99 | PBS PRICE £8.25

Titled after the span of Hannah Hodgson's longest stay in hospital, *163 Days* is an unflinching first full collection from a poet determined to hold the clinical narrative of her medical history to account, and keep her own record. Candid and compelling, Hodgson writes lyrically and with grace. She expresses, "Life today is living inside a flower. / It's knowing that Nursing Homes / don't take under fifties, as if the dead can never start their dying young."

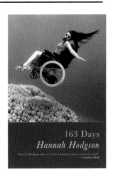

FEB | SEREN | £9.99 | PBS PRICE £7.50

In the Same Light collects 200 poems from the Tang period (618-907 C.E.), which is generally recognised as the golden age of classical Chinese poetry. The editor and translator, Chinese-born, Ireland-based poet Wong May, includes major literary figures like Du Fu as well as lesser-known names like Xu Ning. The compassionate and humble language of Wong's translations offers an intriguing window into a poetic tradition as important today as it was a millennium ago.

JAN | CARCANET | £19.99 | PBS PRICE £15

BOOK REVIEWS

51

STAV POLEG: THE CITY
REVIEWED BY GAZELLE MBA

In Stav Poleg's *The City* we are instructed on how to read. We are told that to read poetry, we must not "expect to understand everything." The reader is urged to cast aside the need to solve the contradictions within a poem or to create a neat paraphrase delineating the poem's true meaning. In its place we hold language differently, not like a "precious vase" we must be careful not to drop, because she reminds us, language is always breaking.

MARCH | CARCANET | £11.99 | PBS PRICE £9.00

PADRAIG REGAN: SOME INTEGRITY

In this Clarissa Luard Prize winning debut the Irish lyric is re-energised, as Regan strives "to see / this & see it clearly." Ekphrastic poems after Rembrandt and Vermeer sit alongside a tribute to the queer victims of the 2016 Orlando Nightclub shootings, and a sequence of wry still lifes which reveal the astonishing breadth and range of this emerging poet. *Some Integrity* is a protean feat of alchemy which celebrates "the gaudy possibilities of language".

JAN | CARCANET | £11.99 | PBS PRICE £9.00

LEONIE RUSHFORTH: DELTAS
REVIEWED BY MAGGIE WONG

The exquisite poems in Leonie Rushforth's debut collection range in setting from the Forbidden City to Moscow's Gorky Park and beyond. These are poems of close observation and generous meditation, attentive to the philosophical as well as the mundane. "Nothing retains its place for long," she writes in the title poem. "Organisms teem, flicker and are gone, / our radical contingency made plain." But *Deltas*, with its soft-spoken intelligence and clear-eyed detail, will surely live on.

PROTOTYPE | £12.00 | PBS PRICE £9.00

DAVID SPITTLE: RUBBLES
REVIEWED BY LEAH JUN OH

In *Rubbles*, poet and filmmaker David Spittle sifts through the post-internet, post-modern and post-apocalyptic – through the "new ruins virtual", to explore the near constant making and unmaking of an uncertain and unsteady present. Spittle aptly uses sonic elements, concrete poetry, and layers of text and image to break the word down to its constituent parts. The connections necessary to build the word/world again are trickier: "touch is now / outmoded, / dangerous and unreal". A provocative and electric read.

MARCH | BROKEN SLEEP BOOKS | £8.99 | PBS PRICE £6.75

ANASTASIA TAYLOR-LIND: ONE LANGUAGE
REVIEWED BY PRAYTUSHA

The debut poetry collection of photo-journalist Anastasia Taylor-Lind, *One Language*, also contains a number of photos. Both the pictures and the poetry stand as witness to the grief and pain of war reportage. Taylor-Lind's style is sparse, tonally suited to the devastating violence she has witnessed. The poems have the sharp focus of a camera lens, "A coffin shaped outline remains at the bottom of an empty hole, / the black satin lining hasn't rotted yet".

MARCH | SMITH/DOORSTOP | £19.99 | PBS PRICE £15

COLM TÓIBÍN: VINEGAR HILL
REVIEWED BY GAZELLE MBA

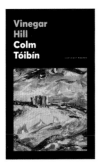

Vinegar Hill is the debut collection from one of Ireland's most celebrated writers, Colm Tóibín. Tóibín's command of poetic form is just as masterful as in his prose, crafting poems characterised by their quiet contemplative air. These poems lay bare the intricacies of family, sexuality and religion, as though they are knots to be patiently untangled. Tóibín speaks of the challenges inherent in venturing into the past in order to understand one's present, when faced with the reluctance of memory, which: "walks towards us, half beckoning."

MARCH | CARCANET | £12.99 | PBS PRICE £9.00

SPRING PAMPHLETS

────── LIAM BATES: MONOMANIAC ──────

In Liam Bates' pamphlet *Monomaniac*, the title of each poem begins with the prefix "mono", with titles from 'Monochrome' to 'Monopolylogue' to 'Monorail'. Within this constraint, Bates' language brings us an unexpected and sparkling portrait of modern life, mental health, and the self. A ring of spring daffodils is a "halo concussion around a cartoon's head" and the air is "hard as guilt." *Monomaniac* is an intriguing work full of colour and humour.

BROKEN   SLEEP   BOOKS | £6.50 |

────── JULIA BIRD: IS, THINKS PEARL ──────

Pearl is the focal, eponymous character in this charming and contemplative pamphlet. Bird explores Pearl's colourful internal and external world with a wistful, kaleidoscopic elegance – and the occasional well-poised stab of darkness. Like its subject, this is a small, precious pamphlet, delving into the experiences of childhood and growing up, the geography of seaside towns and the intense emotional power of places and memories.

EMMA   PRESS | £6.50 |

────── JO MORRIS DIXON: I TOLD YOU EVERYTHING ──────

This urgent, powerfully rhythmic collection throbs from the first page with a feeling of danger and outsider status. Death and youth hold hands in *I Told You Everything*, and growing up is imbued with a sense of peril as these poems navigate puberty, abuse, and homophobia. Dixon's verse is direct, possessing a plain-spoken honesty which is not lacking in evocative, interrogative power.

VERVE   PRESS | £7.50 |

SARALA ESTRUCH: SAY

Sarala Estruch's extraordinary debut pamphlet is unafraid to say the difficult thing. Family history unravels against a cross-cultural backdrop of forbidden marriage, death and grief, as Estruch wrestles to reconcile conflicting identities and an inheritance of trauma, "hurt inflicted on your ancestors / on both sides from both sides". Speaking through this fraught colonial history, *Say* finds a courageous voice of its own and lays the past to rest, albeit restlessly.

FLIPPED   EYE | £4.00 |

HARRY MAN & ENDRE RUSET: UTØYA THEREAFTER

Norwegian poet Endre Ruset and UK poet Harry Man have joined forces on this deeply moving tribute to the victims of the 2011 Utøya massacre in Norway, in which a right-wing extremist killed 69 youngsters. This heartbreaking series of "face poems" memorialises the victims and gives shape to a shared grief. Written with deep empathy and skill, these poems are shot through with violence, but remain "hopeful for more / than a shiverful of calm."

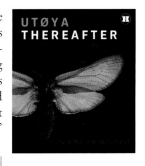

HERCULES   EDITIONS | £10.00 |

NAUSH SABAH: LITANIES

Naush Sabah's new pamphlet *Litanies* uses Sufi prayers and sacred texts as a starting point to explore doubt, dissent and dislocation with lush imagery and an exacting eye. Her poems are both finely chosen and wide-ranging, discussing faith, womanhood, shame, anger, and God. For Sabah "Doubt is the heaviest element with the longest half-life, and there is "in every supplicant a longing, in every believer a silence". This is a pamphlet filled with a complexity that refuses easy answers.

GUILLEMOT   PRESS | £8.00 |

| PAMPHLET REVIEWS

SPRING BOOK LISTINGS

Will Alexander	Refractive Africa	Granta Poetry	£10.99
Moniza Alvi	Fairoz	Bloodaxe Books	£10.99
Martin Anderson	A Country Without Names	Shearsman Books	£10.95
Josephine Balmer	Ghost Passage	Shearsman Books	£10.95
Sarah Barnsley	The Thoughts	The Poetry Business	£10.99
Fiona Benson	Ephemeron	Jonathan Cape	£12.00
Emily Berry	Unexhausted Time	Faber	£10.99
Gavin Bowd	Rifle Song	Red Squirrel Press	£10.00
Alison Brackenbury	Thorpeness	Carcanet Press	£14.99
Annie Brechin	The Mouth of Eulalie	Blue Diode Press	£10.00
Larry Butler	There Are Others	Red Squirrel Press	£10.00
Dawes & Kinsella	UnHistory	Peepal Tree Press	£19.99
Roy Fisher	The Citizen and the making of 'City'	Bloodaxe Books	£14.99
Amali Gunasekera	The Golden Thread	Bloodaxe Books	£10.99
Hannah Hodgson	163 Days	Seren	£9.99
E. P. Jenkins	Rituals	Broken Sleep Books	£7.99
Trevor Ketner	[WHITE]	Broken Sleep Books	£8.99
Bridget Khursheed	The Last Days of Petrol	Shearsman Books	£10.95
Tom Lowenstein	The Bridge at Uji	Shearsman Books	£10.95
John McCullough	Panic Response	Penned in the Margins	£9.99
Andrew McNeillie	Striking a Match in a Storm: Collected Poems	Carcanet Press	£18.99
Arvind Krishna Mehrotra	Collected Poems	Shearsman Books	£14.95
James Peake	The Star in the Branches	Two Rivers Press	£9.99
Carl Philips	Then the War: And Selected Poems 2007-2020	Carcanet Press	£14.99
Stav Poleg	The City	Carcanet Press	£11.99
Lauren Pope	Always Erase	Blue Diode Press	£10
Padraig Regan	Some Integrity	Carcanet Press	£10.99
Denise Riley	Lurex	Picador	£10.99
Leonie Rushforth	Delta	Prototype	£12.00
Lesley Saunders	This Thing of Blood and Love	Two Rivers Press	£9.99
Vernon Scannell	Farewell Performance: Collected Later Poems	Smokestack Books	£9.99
Olive Senior	New and Collected Poems	Carcanet Press	£19.99
Helen Seymour	The Underlook	The Poetry Business	£10.99
Azad Ashim Sharma	ERGASTULUM: Vignettes of Lost Time	Broken Sleep Books	£8.99
Warsan Shire	Bless the Daughter Raised by a Voice in Her...	Chatto &Windus	£12.99
David Spittle	Rubbles	Broken Sleep Books	£8.99
Colm Tóibín	Vinegar Hill	Carcanet Press	£14.99
Anastasia Taylor-Lind	One Language	The Poetry Business	£10.99
Jessica Traynor	Pit Lullabies	Bloodaxe Books	£10.99
Ben Wilkinson	Same Difference	Seren	£9.99
Gerard Woodward	The Vulture	Pan Macmillan	£10.99

TRANSLATIONS

Astrid Alben	Island Mountain Glacier	Prototype	£12.00
Diana Anphimiadi, trans. Jean Sprackland and Nadia Bukia-Peters	Why I No Longer Write Poems (Bilingual Georgian-English edition)	Bloodaxe Books / Poetry Translation Centre	£12.00
Petreus Borel, trans. John Gallas and Kurt Ganz	Rhapsodies	Carcanet Press	£12.99
Ed. Wong May	In the Same Light: 200 Tang Poems	Carcanet Press	£14.99
Pietro De Marchi, trans. Peter Robinson	Reports after the Fire (Bilingual Italian-English edition)	Shearsman Books	£12.95
Louis de Paor, trans. Kevin Anderson and Biddy Jenkinson	Crooked Love / Grá fiar (Bilingual English-Irish edition)	Bloodaxe Books	£12.00
Philip Terry	Lascaux Notebook: Ice Age Poetry	Carcanet Press	£14.99